Why He Won't Marry YOU

Things the right man will tell you and the wrong one doesn't want you to find out.

JONATHAN K. SANDERS

WHY HE WON'T MARRY YOU

Copyright ©2017 by Jonathan Sanders

ISBN: 978-0-692-92598-0
Printed in the United States of America

Book design by Cheryl Holland
A'Sista Media Group, LLC

ACKNOWLEDGMENTS

To those who influenced me the most, Bishop Fred and my late mother, Queen Esther Sanders, I offer the most sincere gratitude. The words you spoke to me, speak in my spirit and remind me that this is just the beginning. To my wonderful sons Jonathan and Joshua, you bring me joy. The world awaits you, as you await the world. Continue to prove to me, and others, that you are the men that your mother and I raised.

Introduction

One of the reasons why I wrote this book, is because I kept hearing women, and people in general, say that black men don't want to be married. That is far from the truth. I have been all around the world and divorced for the last 12 years. My mother, whom I affectionately call 'Queen Esther', told me years ago before she left earth, "Son, I may not be around to see you get married again but remember this, there's a difference between quantity and quality. You can have a room full of women but you can also have a room full of no good women. It's the same with men. Remember, I told you son." Mama, you ain't never lied! These days it's never about quantity but always about quality! I am 47 now, but I can still remember traveling the world with my father as a younger man and him telling me to look at how beautiful some, certainly not all, women were from head to toe. There are some who have their hair flawless, body immaculate, nails done, and their teeth are perfect! They even have their own businesses, cars, and homes; yet they don't even have a man, let alone a husband. Something just might be wrong somewhere.

My father would say, "How can a woman have all of that, yet there's no man in sight? Trust me! If you see a beautiful woman who has accomplished great success, with looks to match, but no man, something has to be terribly wrong!" Of course, I'm not talking about the woman that is enjoying her singleness and does not want to be in a relationship at the time. That's a whole different subject. Now my sister, if you want to continue to blame Terrell, Dexter, and Larry, as to the reason why you don't have a man, that's fine. With that said, you may want to put this book down now because I'm getting ready to go where the average man won't. Let me ask you a question…have you ever dated a man for several years, ended the relationship, and then found out that man you were dating all those years got married to someone else less than six months later? Say what you want, but if that was me, I would feel some kind of way. That does not mean that there was something wrong with you. There could have been something wrong with him, or maybe the two of you were just not a good match. Regardless, this kind of situation will certainly raise an eyebrow or two. I by no means am an expert on women. God knows I'm not. I had a beautiful marriage for 13 years and then things went bad. Yet, I have learned that life goes on. I've traveled all over the world and dated some of God's finest creatures. Though I do not have all of the answers, I have learned many things that I would like to share with you. This book is not written to put any woman down. Absolutely not! I would never disrespect God's chosen vessels that are female. I was raised by a beautiful mother who is now in heaven. I believe she is continuing to look down on me, waiting to see what I will do with all the knowledge and wisdom she invested in me. This is why I write to you, my friends. I have three beautiful chocolate sisters whom I love and greatly adore and want nothing but the best for them, and also for you. Give me a chance before you cut me off, tune me out, or unplug me. Just read what I have to say. I myself, like many men, would love to get up early on a Tuesday morning and go down to the jewelry store and pick out the most beautiful diamond in the showcase. I would love to arrange a secret engagement party with our closest friends and family members. I would like to get down on one knee and propose to the queen of my dreams, hoping God will make it last forever. Maybe all I had was one chance. Then again, maybe I will find love again and it will be even better the second time around. Let me open my heart, expose my feelings, give you a piece of my mind, and share with you what I believe are some of the issues that are holding women back from the man of their dreams. Give me a chance to share what I know and remember. If this doesn't bless you, I'll buy the book back. Thank you for sharing your time with me.

TABLE OF CONTENTS

Chapter 1 - It has nothing to do with you. He's just not ready.
» *His last relationship was hell*
» *His ex-wife or ex-girlfriend has him in debt*
» *He's having fun and enjoying the single life*
» *Atlanta*

Chapter 2 - You're too independent and far too bossy
» *Female CEO's, Supervisors, and Managers*
» *He can't tell you anything because you already know it all*
» *Woman, you aren't my momma. Stop trying to control me!*
» *Submission. That dreaded word*
» *The Philippines*

Chapter 3 - Loose lips sink ships.
» *You can't control your tongue*
» *Your mouth is wicked and you're way too disrespectful*
» *There are some things you just don't say to a man*

Chapter 4 – Twenty-Four Hour Church Girl
» *There are times when that man doesn't want to hear anything about God and that doesn't make him the devil*
» *You listen to your pastor more than you listen to him*

Chapter 5 - You're a lady in the streets and in the sheets. You are no longer a freak!
» *What one woman won't do another one will*
» *Be a woman that will satisfy her husband, no matter what*
» *I miss the old school church mothers*
» *Don't ask your father or pastor, but ask him what he likes*

Chapter 6 - You are damaged goods from your previous relationship(s) and it shows.

» *You need time to heal*
» *Stop talking bad about your ex*
» *Marriage is not one of your requirements*
» *You are content being single, especially after all the hell you've been through*

Chapter 7 - You're full of drama and have too much attitude(Ms. Drama & Stacy Attitude)

» *Misplaced affections*
» *Attitude determines altitude*
» *Black women and reality TV*
» *Stop telling your business on social media*

Chapter 8 - You are fine but don't have a dime!

» *Don't expect him to have what you don't have*
» *Finance without romance is a nuisance!*
» *You're broke with no change ($) in sight!*

Chapter 9 - You are not the marrying type

» *Men date hoes, but they'll never marry them*
» *Whatever you do, don't give it up on the first date*
» *Girl, who taught you how to do that? The freaks come out at night*

Chapter 10 - He likes peanut butter and jelly!

» *Simply put, he's gay or bisexual.*

Chapter 11 - He's a player!

» *At this junction of his life all he wants to do is play.*
» *Stop trying to change him because he'll change only when he's ready*
» *If you play his game, be sure you know the rules*

Chapter 12 - He's already married
» *The kind of woman that wants what she's not supposed to have*
» *The thirst is real*
» *Leave that married man alone*

Chapter 13 - He didn't marry you in the time you've given him
» *Whose time table are you going by? Your's only? Why not his too?*
» *Is there compatibility, or are you fighting and not getting along?*
» *If the relationship is still together, there is hope*

Chapter One

It has absolutely NOTHING to do with you. He's just not ready.

- *His last relationship was hell*
- *His ex-wife and kids has him in debt.*
- *He's having fun and enjoying the single life.*
- *Atlanta*

It has absolutely, positively, nothing to do with you. He's simply just not ready. There may be many reasons why, but the fact remains that if he's not ready, he's just not ready. So many women think that there is something wrong with them, but that's far from the truth. I've seen women go to the salon and get long hair and then a week later it's short. Then go blonde for two weeks, then change it to brown, then back to black, all in the span of three weeks. Some foolishly think that there is something wrong with the way they look. Some have even gone as far as going to see the doctor and getting fake breasts, fake booty, lips, and even hips, and that man still doesn't want to walk down the aisle. Simply because it has nothing to do with you. With men, it doesn't take a whole lot of reasons to make him doubt your marriage will work. All it takes is one. Some have sworn to never get married, while some boast of being in the "one and done club." They claim that they will never re-marry. Maybe he's divorced and rebounding from a bad marriage or maybe he saw what his parents went through trying to hold a bad marriage together. He may just not want to go down that road and feels it is best to leave well enough alone and stay single.

You can wash his boxers, fry his chicken and fish, along with the mac-n-cheese and collard greens! You can love him like no other, to the point his toes twinkle and curl up to the sky above! If he's not ready, he's just not ready, so none of that means anything! There may be a plethora of reasons why he is hesitant, but by no means think that it has anything to do with you. Your frustrations may have caused you to look at yourself and even ask your girlfriends if there something is wrong with you. If you do that, you are looking in the wrong direction because it's not you, it's him. How many men and women do I know that have soaked their pillows with tears thinking what's wrong with me? Do I not look good enough and am I not pretty enough? Is it because of the children I already have? What is it about me that he doesn't choose me? Nothing! The brother is just not ready. Let me say something very plain but so complex to others. The number one way that you would know a man is not ready is by asking him! You don't have to go to church and ask the preacher what they see in your future. You don't need to call up a 1-900 number and speak to a psychic. Neither do you have to wait for a dream or vision. Most likely, ninety percent of the time, he will tell you. But only if you ask him! The question is, are you listening to his response? Most women (certainly not all) would go by the actions of the man, versus what he verbally says. Huge mistake! When it comes to men they usually say what they mean. He'll get comfortable with hanging out with you all the time but he knows if he already told you he's not ready for a relationship, don't expect anything different. Just like women get comfortable in the relationship, so do men. He will take you out of town, around his friends, and maybe even to his mother's house for dinner. But if he said to you verbally, especially over and over again, that he doesn't want to get married, believe what he says not just what he does. The flip side to this is that there are many women that feel exactly the same way. They have been in abusive relationships with a man who has physically hurt them, left them with children and won't pay child support, slept with her girlfriends, and the list goes on. She's done! And there's nothing wrong with that because everyone is entitled to their choice. In relationships, the worst thing you can lose is your voice and your choice. You might as well be a mute robot!

I can't tell you how many women I know, who have told me after two years on and off with a man, he kept on saying he didn't want to get married but they thought they could change him. You have to go by what he is saying and not only what he is doing. Please don't ever forget that. I didn't even bring up the fact that he may know that he's a "dog" and he is trying to save your heart from heartbreak. He may know that he can't be faithful, and isn't even planning on trying, so he figures, why string you along? Why jack your heart up? He knows that he is not the perfect man that you think he is and that you think you want to be with for the rest of your life. He has his own issues to deal with and probably many of them. Especially when he knows that he has a whole bunch of skeletons in his closet, under his bed and in the trunk of his car! The "dog of a man" that he may be today is nothing compared to the awesome man that he sees himself to be in the future. He's just not there yet. He could be saving you from the biggest heartbreak of your life! I've known women that knew the man was no good. Matter of fact his momma told her he was no good, yet she chose to stay right by his side thinking she's going to change him. I know I may not get any points on this statement but I'll say it anyhow. I think a woman should applaud a man that backs out of a marriage because he knows he can't and won't be faithful. Do you know how many men go ahead and get married anyway and know they are going to cheat? Do you really think that marriage makes a man be faithful? Really? No way. You don't even believe that. I truly believe that it takes a whole lot of time to become a quality man. Great, faithful, and loyal men are not made overnight. It usually comes from them getting all of the "play" out of themselves and then when they get in their "seasoned age," their qualities begin to stand up. Men have a lot of "play" in them, especially at younger ages. Some men don't come into their greatness until further down the road in age and in life. In an average city, there are more women than men. Do all men cheat? Of course not. But they certainly have the potential, the access, and the ego to do it, if it's in them to.

Atlanta is known to bachelors as a "player's paradise." There are several reasons why. This city is full of successful single women and a bunch of gay men! Now before your attack back, those that know about the "real-real," you know I'm telling the straight-up truth! But let me get to the subject at hand. "Hot-lanta" has so many athletes, actresses, rappers, and the list goes on. I have many friends and some family there and a few of them are bachelors. They act like they are on the south-side of heaven. Lol. Hear me and pay as close of attention as you can. Some men know that in certain areas there's a shortage of men and they will use this to their advantage. They have women putting their clothes in the cleaners, getting their haircut, paying car notes, and even paying rent and mortgages! All because she's gotta have it, and you know what it is. I wish I was lying but I'm not. And no matter where you are, there's always a desperate, thirsty woman, willing to do all those things and so much more just to have a man, even if he's a bad one! Can you be honest and agree with me? Depending on the age or stage that they are at in life, some men are really just focused on having fun from their perspective. If you like seafood, Oceanaire Seafood on Peachtree Street is the place to go. You will see a lot of influential people there. If you like "soul food" then you would want to go to Ray's on the River located down on Powers Ferry Road. If you love music, especially jazz and nice scenery to get to know somebody, I'm told that this is the place to be. I have been told that sitting on the dock along the Chattahoochee River, taking in serene views and enjoying a full menu of Ray's dishes, is like a night in "Chocolate Heaven." I mentioned Atlanta, but of course, it can also be Los Angeles, Chicago, Detroit, or even New York City. "Players" are everywhere and where you least expect. Not giving them a rite of passage but many of them have their own insidious reasons to play. Some of them are fresh out of a bad breakup, while others are just ending a long rough marriage. There are those that are working jobs which requires them to travel, so they choose not to settle down because they don't do long distance relationships. The fact of the matter is when a man wants to play, that's exactly what he will do, play. You can't stop him. You can get the password to his phone, you can crack the code to his email and even find out what he's doing on social media. None of that means anything if it's in his heart to play. This is where wise women that have common sense come in. You say to yourself, if that's what he wants to do then let him do that. What is crazy is that I have known women who date men that they know are players, in hopes that they could 'lasso' them into marriage. They catch him in his mess over and over again and still stay with him. They hide in the bushes and follow him like an undercover agent on CSI Los Angeles! After they've done all of that and found him out to be cheating, lying, and playing low down dirty shame games, guess what? They are still right there waiting for a change that will never come! All the time saying God is able. Po' thang. God is able to help you do what you don't want to do, not what you want to keep on doing. It looks like somebody just wasted a whole bunch of their time, resources, and money for nothing at all. If he wants to play girlfriend, let that ninja play. Just make sure you don't sign up for his games! At the end of the day, do you really want a mate that would rather play than stay? My point exactly. The fact of the matter is, some men are just not the marrying type. The sooner you learn that the smoother life will be.

Chaper Two

You're too independent and far too bossy.

- *Female CEOs, Supervisor's, and Managers*
- *He can't tell you anything because you already know it all.*
- *Woman you aren't my momma. Stop trying to control me!*
- *Submission. That dreaded word.*
- *The Philippines*

If I hear one more woman say "I don't need a man," I'm going to explode. It seems like that's the lingo of independent single women today. I understand clearly that you have your own job, your own business, your own career, and you're making things happen for yourself. That's a wonderful thing. But please my sister, hear me when I tell you this, don't let the man that's interested in you hear that come out of your mouth. When I hear a woman say that, it comes off so crazy because they act like they don't want a man, but in actuality they really do. I'm not talking about the sister who was just burned by the brother who tore up her credit and left her with two babies and no child support. I'm talking about sisters that inwardly desire a man.

Well, I'm getting ready to lose some female friends but I just have to keep it real. I did a personal survey and I asked about six friends and family members what was, or rather who was, your worst boss. Unanimously, they all said black females. Wow! Personally, I would say the exact same thing. Now before you turn this book sideways and burn it with the lighter you got from Las Vegas when you were on vacation, please let me explain. Lord knows that I'm not talking about all black women, just a few. Some have to let you know that they're in charge every other hour. Some will boss you around like you're Kunta Kinte on the chicken farm down in Georgia. I mean, they just have to let the power that they have be shown. It's obvious that they've never been in a leadership position before because real power does not have to be flaunted in the face of others. There's nothing like power that's not seen. And there's nothing like a woman that has authority, yet doesn't feel that they have to flaunt it. I'm so glad that I'm certainly not talking about ALL black women or women period. Absolutely not! We have some sisters that have so much confidence and self-esteem, that they will never demean another, no matter what! A woman with power and authority, who is yet humble, meek, and laid-back, is rare in this new culture that we live in.

There is a story in the Bible about a rich King named Xerxes who was throwing a party and he asked his wife, Queen Vashti, to come down to his party so all his friends could see how fine she was. She was a very, very, beautiful woman. Believe it or not, she dissed him hard right in front of all his friends and said, "I'm not coming!" He was so upset that he literally cut her off right then and there. All the man wanted her to do is come down to his party so all his friends could see how beautiful she was, but she wouldn't even do that. She was busy with her girls having a party of her own. That day, he changed the law of that country and said that women can't do that to their husbands. Other politicians of his town had told him that if the king's wife can get away with that that type of behavior, it would spread all throughout the country and cause havoc in marriages and relationships. This is why the king had to change the law. He banished her from ever even seeing him again. That's how we got the story of Queen Esther.

Xerxes had a countrywide beauty pageant held for the next woman that would take her place, and we know that woman was Esther. Come on sisters, work with me, work with me. That may not seem like much to you, but that was a big blow to that man's ego. And he was the King! Can you imagine how insulting that was to him? This woman didn't have to work, cook, or clean, just simply be the queen and be there for her King, but she couldn't even do that. Her independence and arrogance cost her the marriage and lavish lifestyle.

Say what you want, but that's a powerful lesson for all to learn. Don't be the kind of woman that a man can't tell you anything. Him taking the lead doesn't always mean he is trying to be demeaning or flaunt authority over you. When you see a couple working together in agreement and no one is wrestling for the power to be in charge, you see a beautiful thing.

Let the man be the boss. And you know, actually, I said that wrong, you shouldn't let him be the boss, he is the boss, according to nature, as well as the Bible. It declares God the head of Christ, Christ the head of man, and man the head of woman. Now before you take this book and throw it in a fireplace or the trash can…stop, hold up, wait a minute. I'm not talking about any man, I'm talking about a man worth submitting to. There is a major difference between the two! I don't have to go any further right there because a real woman knows exactly what I'm talking about. One that you can see in your future. One that you can see yourself being married to and calling him your king as he calls you his queen. Not a "buster" riding shotgun in his homies car and don't have a pot to piss in or a window to throw it out of. I'm certainly not referencing all men in this matter, just one that you can find yourself submitting to. That's what I'm talking about.

One of the worse things to see is a woman bossing a man around. Don't try to be his mother, be his companion. Most men will greatly rebel when they see a woman trying to put handcuffs on them of any kind. I once had a friend whose wife literally timed him when he would go to the store. She would say, "It only takes ten minutes to get there, ten minutes to get back, and I'll add five minutes just in case there's traffic. But if you are longer than twenty-five minutes, it's going to be World War III when you get back home!" What? Now that right there is crazy. No man wants to be married to a parole officer, probation officer, or especially a time management specialist.

Submission simply means accepting or yielding to a superior force or authority of another person. It also comes from the word submarine, simply meaning, to come under the mission and the assignment of another. I know some women that act like this word is hot lava from a volcano in Hawaii! If you even form the words submission, they are ready to slap you in your upper lip. They say they will never be under the authority of no man or anybody. I understand this to a point because they are some that have given up their authority and put it in the hands of the wrong man who took it for granted.

Because of that, they have refused to yield their authority over to another simply because of what that one man did. But why take it out on the next man what that last man did to you? That is totally unfair. Understandable, but unfair. If you believe that you have met a man who is somebody that you can see in your future, submission will become the least of your problems.

In 1988 while serving in the US Marine Corps I trained in the place called Subic Bay, Philippines. I was only around 18 years old and was in for the shock of my life. There were some other Marines who kind of took me under their wing like a younger brother and they begin to show me around all around that fascinating country. One of the first things they taught and showed me was, yep you got it, women. Come on now I was only eighteen years old in another country and I guess you could say that I was sowing my wild oats. They began to tell me that Filipino women are extremely submissive and will literally do anything you want. Let me say that again, *anything* you want. They were literally no holds barred. Now get your mind out the gutter because I'm not just talking about in one aspect of life. They would wash all your clothes and I mean scrub your drawers until they were as white as the clouds in heaven. They would wash you up from your head to your feet and from the 'rooter to the tooter'. Some literally would even brush your teeth. If I'm lying, I'm flying, and my feet haven't left the floor! You can only imagine what this did to my adolescent mind. I had never been exposed to anything like this. I had never even seen it anything like it. Maybe in the movies growing up, but I did not believe these kind of women existed. So many of my friends were in strong long relationships with these women and a great deal of them even married these Filipino women, brought them back to the United States and had many children. Wow! It was said that a lot of these women were taught to serve their men by their mothers and grandmothers in hopes of a better world and better life for them in the U.S. I found this to be very true. When that man would marry that woman, she would somehow get her mother to come to the U.S. and sometimes even other relatives. These women with their submitted ways we're blowing brother's minds literally. Our other friends who were stationed back in the States ,when we would call and tell them how we were living in the Philippines, did everything they could to get stationed over there. We would send pictures back home that were literally breathtaking, making our buddies jealous. Those were some fun times which made us idols in their eyes. There was one young "main hottie," who became my girlfriend there and believe it or not I thought I was in love. She treated me like I was the Prince of Zamunda! She did just about everything for me except put red roses petals at my feet when I woke up in the morning! When I would stay at her house on the weekends she would cook me breakfast, lunch, and dinner. She washed all my clothes and I promise you she even ironed my socks and underwear, by hand. When I put them on and walked down the street it felt like I had a bulletproof vest on. She starched them too! Lol. Hilarious. Man, you couldn't tell me that I was not in love. I told my mom about her and I'll never forget it. I think about it now. I would call my mom and tell her how good she was treating me and my mom would just listen. She didn't say too much at all, she would just listen. I'll never forget sending my mom some pictures of me and my Filipino 'boo'. I told my mom that I really, really, liked this girl and wanted to bring her back home with me. My mother responded in a way that makes me bust out laughing to this day. You know what she said? "Boy don't play with me! You're not in love! You're just having a lot of hot sex!" Hot sex? What's that? Lol. But you know what? Mom was right. I was just caught up, with my head in the clouds and I was being swept off my feet by her submissive ways. You talking about caught up! A ninja was caught up! How do you know, you ask? Because I still have Linda's pictures to this day. Shhh. Don't tell nobody! I don't know a man alive that is not attracted to a submissive woman. Oh man, there's just something about it, that's hard to explain. Maybe you have to be a man to understand it. When a man knows he has a woman that will submit to him in every way, I guarantee you he won't be letting her out of his sight. Trust me.

Chapter Three

Loose lips sink ships.

- *You can't control your tongue.*
- *Your mouth is wicked and you're way too disrespectful.*
- *There are some things you just don't say to a man.*

We live in a culture now where a woman will put a man in check quick! Some 'sistahs' will say it right in his face with her hand on her hip, gladly giving him a piece of her mind. I simply believe that a classy woman knows how to say what you need to say to a man, but will never lose her classiness. Believe it or not, growing up as a child, I never really saw my mother and father argue. Now, I'm pretty sure they did, but they never did it around us as children. Of course, I'm sure he did many things that got on her nerves. I mean come on, he was a preacher! I never saw her belittle him or put him down, especially in public. You may not believe me, but a man's ego is as fragile as a dozen of eggs from Walmart. Sometimes, if a woman says certain things to a man that bruise his ego, he will never ever forget it. There is also a chance that he will never look at you the same. "You don't make enough money, you don't look that handsome, my ex made love to me much better than you did with your little dick!" Wow! Now, wait one whole minute! Come on sister that is cruel! That's what you call some low blows and emasculation of a man. But sad to say it, that's how some women flow today. They'll say what they want to whomever they want and that's just how it is. It can be her father, her boss, the male police officer who pulled her over for speeding or the pastor. This type of woman bites her lip for no one. Whew. Dangerous.

Years ago, I dated a young lady and I was really bonding with her and we were getting along very, very, well. Like any other couple that is learning each other, we had our share of arguments, but one argument stands out among them all. We were at the food court in the mall with three other couples and she got upset with me about something very small and straight up unloaded on a brother. She brought out some personal things up loudly and right in front of our friends. I was shocked because we were really getting along and I thought I had a future with her. I had never seen this side of her or seen her blow up like that. You do know, they say if you want to know how a person feels about you let them get real mad and see what words come out of their mouth. I had just bought her an $800 tennis bracelet. It may not seem like a lot of money to you, but at the time that was a whole whole lot to me. Always remember when a man spends money on you, sometimes it's because he sees you in his future. I mean the things she said floored me to the point that I don't even want to repeat them now. After such a low blow, I really could never look at her the same. She apologized and we tried to move past it the next few weeks, but unfortunately the relationship ended. In relationships, at times, it can take one bad incident to happen and that couple can never get back to where they were. That was the ax to the bottom of the tree in that relationship.

I'll never forget, years ago, I was at a pool hall and a woman and her man were in an argument. He seemed to try to keep it quiet between the two of them in the corner, but she got louder and louder. She started cussing him out, putting her fingers all in his face and going off. Not to mention that she was about 5 feet tall and he was about 6'5, weighing 300 pounds. Everybody stopped and looked at them arguing. She did everything in her little power to make him go off or hit her, but he never did. I don't know if he was used to her behavior or knew Jesus and kept his cool. Thank God, he didn't have a temper! That is so foolish of a woman to do that to a man in today's society. These men in these streets don't normally have that type of tolerance. Hitting women is normal for some men today. Their hands are bisexual. They hit men and women.

Chapter Four

24 Hour Church Girl

- *There are times when that man doesn't want to hear anything about God, and that doesn't make him the devil*

- *You listen to your pastor more than you do him*

Alright, alright. I know that this is going to be a hot and taboo subject for most, but I'm up for the challenge. This chapter covers the behavior of a lot of 'church women' that make church their whole life. They talk about what's going on at the church, their ministry, prophecies and dreams they've had. The whole conversation is about church, church, church. At the restaurant, they're talking about church and not the food. At the mall, they're talking about ministry and not the clothes. They are obsessed with the church. Here you are with this man that has taken you out on a date downtown at a five-star restaurant to dine and enjoy one another, but instead of him leading the conversation, you grabbed the mic and started talking about church. Some even have the nerve to bless the food and start speaking in tongues at the table! Hetabalo-ishe-key! Those are her holy tongues. A hot mess! Lmbbo!

I have personally found that there are a lot of women ministers who've sunk themselves into this kind of life. Say what you want to say, but God never intended for a woman to *only* be a pastor, preacher, evangelist, or prophetess. Perhaps he also wanted her to be a wife, a companion, a sister, a friend, someone to share life with. There's much more to life than just church. Tell God I said that! Smile.

It's sad to see so many women in church lose their marriages or relationships because they dove into ministry and church fanaticism. Some didn't even have a ministry until their relationship broke up, so now ministry is like that new companion. Definitely awkward. This is far more predominant when it comes to female ministers, which I certainly have nothing against. Many of them have great balance in their lives and they know how to separate church from their regular lives. They are very well balanced. But trust and believe me when I tell you, there are a lot of single church women that don't know how to talk about anything other than church. These are the ones that have dreams and say that God told them a certain man was their husband. Today it's getting a real crazy with that. They say God told them this and God told them that. As a matter of fact, God speaks to them like every five minutes. I told one prophetess,

"You and God must be Facebook friends because he talks to you all the time!" Yes, I did! No man wants to hear church talk no matter how good God has been. Holy women are certainly high on the totem pole and in great demand. Yet balance is the key to life. Serve him, praise him, and speak well of the good Lord, but definitely, have that balance.

The poor man can't get you to fry him an egg sandwich, but your pastor got you making him or her steak, mashed potatoes, sautéed green beans, and grandma's old fashioned Kool-Aid! The devil is a lie! I could never understand how some women would do so much for their pastor and so little for the man in their lives. If he is wise, the man you are dating will detect that quickly and have a problem with it. I think it's a wonderful thing to serve God's leaders, but not at the expense of the man in your life. I must reiterate that I'm not speaking about just any man, but rather a fiancé or someone you believe will remain a part of your life. You shouldn't spend all your free time after work just doing the things for the church because your Pastor asked you, and never spend time with a love interest that has great future potential. I'm getting ready to hit you with something, so don't duck. There are some pastors that love to have single women in their church because they know they have a lot of free time. When these type of pastors see a woman talking and courting a man they will get very jealous. Without even meeting or speaking to the man, they'll tell you God isn't in it. Pastor, please! That's the oldest trick in the book. He want's you all to himself because you being single will further his agenda. As bad as that sounds, let's hope his agenda is just church! Remember I told you.

Chapter Five

You're a lady in the streets and in the sheets. You are no longer a freak.

- *What one woman won't do another one will!*
- *Be a woman that will satisfy her husband no matter what*
- *I miss the old school church mothers*
- *Don't just ask your father or pastor, but ask your man what he likes*
- *You'd be surprised at what you can learn to like especially when it's for the one you love*

Now, let me first and foremost get this out of the way. To everyone that is reading this book, I may not be referring to your husband, but rather your boyfriend. I don't have to tell you what the scriptures say concerning premarital sex. I'm sure you are grown and you know what's up. Let me drop it on you like this, I'm a blogger and I talk about all types of topics concerning relationships. I once wrote a post about Christians and premarital sex and things really opened in that dialogue. It went like this. A survey was taken among believers and the question was asked: In a moment of weakness you and your fiance had sex and you found out the sex was horrible. The worst ever. Would you stay engaged and marry them? A whopping majority said emphatically, NO! Whether you want to be real or not, sex has and always will be extremely important in relationships to both men and women. If you don't believe me, ask people that you know who will tell you the truth. Then after you ask them, ask yourself! So can I continue? I believe I will!

I grew up with three beautiful sisters. Two of them are hair stylists and have a very popular hair salon in town. I enjoy going there at times and hearing the many things that women talk about, normally when men are not around. I even hang around to hear what some of those things are and have actually raised my hand and asked some questions. Many have been raised in what you would call straight up strict religious homes. Their parents told them certain things were ungodly. Yet most of these things they were told were not biblical, but were simply traditional ideals on what they thought was right and wrong. All advice is not good advice, no matter who it comes from. People have a tendency of wanting to vicariously live their lives through others. What has happened is that many women have gotten so *super* holy that they buried the freak in themselves. Oh, but it's still in there. And God didn't take that away, because he knew that her man would like that. Yes! I said it. We all know that the bible says "marriage is honorable and the bed undefiled," but that scripture has been misinterpreted. Now, that doesn't mean that just anything goes, yet it doesn't mean you can't sexually please each other. I'm not here to preach to you, but merely give you some advice and then I'll leave the rest for your pastor. Remember, a lot of our parents were taught to restrain their love making and sexuality. Yet, we know today the chains are off and people are buck wild and free.

This is why I believe that you should have premarital counseling and discuss some of the things that you and your future husband would and would not do in your bedchamber before you get married. Once you find out these things, then you will truly know if this is the kind of person that you want to be with for the rest of your life and if you will be able to enjoy lovemaking with them. If he's a sensible man, it is most likely that he will not want you to do anything that will be out of your league. Just don't be a woman that comes to the bedroom with a list of restrictions on what you won't do without hearing the brother out. Whatever your restrictions are, you should at least sit down and talk with him to make sure that you will be sexually compatible. Sometimes the man has told the woman what he likes and she starts off doing it during the dating stage. But once the ring is on her finger, it's a whole new ball game. I don't care what anybody says, in my personal opinion, that's a straight-up sex trap. Have you ever heard a spouse say that when they were dating their mate used to do whatever for them all night long, but after they married they only get it on Christmas and their birthday? Too pitiful. Lol. But on the real, that's a crying shame. What you did to get him, you should do to keep him. Not counting the fact, that what you won't do, the next woman will and will do it with all her might! Don't get mad at me, I'm just telling you the truth.

I so miss the old school church mothers. You see, back in the day, church mother's didn't only help in the church, but they also helped the young girls in their families, schools, and in the neighborhoods. An hour conversation with a church mother at the family reunion would be like talking to a psychiatrist and counselor. They were your mother and mine or our aunts, if you please. They were very old but full of great wisdom. I'm talking about the kind of wisdom that you don't find in books or even in some of our colleges. These women just knew what to do and when to do it! They would teach the young women on how to deal with their men. They would teach them how to cook the best of meals and keep a very immaculately clean house. I mean, even if you just look at the church you can tell that the pendulum has shifted. The church mothers seem to be missed greatly. There seems to be a new school of church mamas that have come in the house. These new church mamas look like they left the jazz club wearing three rings on each hand and Salt and Pepa hoop earrings! Extra long hair, loud colored hair, and a dress that looks like it was spray-painted on! Yes, these new mamas are working out at the YMCA, playing tennis, or in a bicycle riding club, and they want you to know it baby! You can't tell these new mamas nothing! Lol. If they bent over to pick up something, you might see their thongs! A mess. Older mothers are now coming to church with the man they met at bingo last month believing God can save him. Lol. Kind of comical but it's surely the truth. The younger women and new wives no longer have that old school influence that once was. Some, unfortunately, are going to the internet and reality TV looking for ways to keep that man satisfied. Well at least she's trying and that's always a good sign.

Years ago I was speaking at a church in Louisville, Kentucky. We had a wonderful program that evening. I will never forget this to the day I die. A young lady came up to me after service who appeared to be in her mid 30s. She said, "You seem to be a man of great knowledge and wisdom and I want to ask you a question." She said that she was married and her husband loved oral sex but her pastor said they should not do that because it's against the word of God. She was torn. "What should I do sir, I'm so confused." I was literally blown away! I had never had this happen to me. I began to fumble and was confused because here it is a woman is wanting to please her husband, but also wanting to obey her pastor. "What should I tell her," I asked myself. I told her it was late and I'd get back to her. I was scheduled to be there for about three days, so I had time to think and figure this thing out. I walked away in bewilderment because that was a great, great challenge. On the third night, she came back to me and to be quite honest, I really tried to avoid her. But because she asked me I gave her an answer. Well sort of. I said to her, "My sister, let me ask you this. What would you rather have, a happy pastor or a happy husband?" I ended the conversation just like that and walked away. Let me say something that many of you may not agree with, but it is what it is. You have some pastors today that are so controlling that they will tell you their opinion of the word of God and not the word of God itself. My own pastor told me years ago, "Son when the Bible stops speaking, you stop speaking. Don't add to it or take away from it. I couldn't agree more!" To this day, I haven't found one scripture that says a woman could not please her husband in that way. Maybe I'm naive, so if you know that scripture please holla at a brother! Let me drop this on you before I go to my next subject. A young church lady came up to me and said, "My husband wants me to hide in our house and when he finds me, he wants to tie me up then make love to me! Do you think that would be okay? What does the Bible say about role playing?" I responded "I don't see in the scriptures where you can't! Ask

God not me! Lol." I do know one thing. I would feel some type of way as a husband if my bedroom was regulated by what the bishop said and not what I said. I wouldn't want a wife that is controlled and dictated to, in that fashion. That pastor is sounding more like a pimp than a preacher if he controls what the women in his church do with their own husbands. That's my story and I'm sticking to it.

I really don't want to say this, but I'm compelled to. In my profession, this is one of the biggest deal breakers when it comes to sexual compatibility. This question is asked by women all over. How far do I go when it comes to satisfying my companion? You sisters that are reading this, I'm going to pretend that you are asking ME. Now before I respond, you must know this. This question varies by who you ask. Remember that. If you ask your pastor, your father, your brother, and even your man, most likely ALL of them will have a different answer! Believe that!

We now live in a day of sexual freedom, sexual immorality, swingers, and dingers! In other words, we live in a culture of straight up sexual freaks! I don't know who this is for, but you better know what and who you're getting involved with when it comes to marriage. Menage a trois seem to be the norm among even married couples today. It started with top Hollywood actors, actresses, and singers, but now anything can go, even with an average married couple. Some couples even go to swinger parties with the intent to have sex with other couples while watching their mate in the act. In my opinion, that is absolutely nuts! For a husband to watch his wife get 'banged' by another man and sit there with a drink enjoying it, is crazy! For a wife to willingly smile in amazement while another woman rides her husband like a Dallas Cowgirl, is bananas! Yet this is normal behavior in our society today. One brother at the pool hall said he was into choking and whipping his women. I was shocked! One of the other fellas said he didn't believe him until old dude pulled out his phone. He showed pictures of the women loving it and even showed texts of women literally asking for him to do that. Absolutely unreal! Now don't ask me why I was there! Just get my point. You have to absolutely know what you're getting into because if you don't, it may cost you a life of misery. Certainly to each his or her own. I cannot force my beliefs or opinions on anyone so at the end of the day, we all have to do what we think is best!

You remember that old song, "I Can't Get No Satisfaction?" This is the cry of a lot of men that I talk to. They say they have a good woman. She can cook, she can clean, and even takes care of the children, but when it comes to the lovin' she doesn't satisfy him. Now I'm not talking about somebody that's a straight up freak and no matter what you attempt to do it's never enough. I know that there are some men, that no matter what you do, they can't be satisfied. In church, that's called having a lust demon. There are some men that have dissatisfaction that has nothing to do with you. It's their insatiable desire for sex that is completely overbearing. Some men can get a good woman, but lose her by going crazy in the bedroom. They will have you swinging from the chandelier, dressed up like Catwoman, and still won't be satisfied. Lol. Leave him alone or take him to Jesus, the preference is yours. Choose wisely. If it's someone you believe in a future with, ask what satisfies him, and at the right time, satisfy him with all your might! I was at a women's conference years ago at a church. I heard an old school church mother teaching. She addressed the married women. She told them, "If his thing goes up, it's your job to take it back down. Remember don't let a hungry man leave the house. If you do, he's going to get fed somewhere." Go ahead mother and teach!

I'm back at it. What would you rather have? A happy pastor or a happy husband? This is why you don't necessarily have to ask your pastor how to love your husband. Ask your husband. Ask, "Big Daddy, how do you want it?" There are many controlling dictator type of pastors out there that try to tell married couples in their congregations what they should do and not do to and with their husbands. Now, I'm about to get in some big trouble with this one here, but that's alright because I know how to get out. You could be sitting under a boring, lackadaisical, laid-back, sexually unresponsive pastor, who only believes that the missionary style of sex is the only one God approves of. That is the furthest from the truth! You can also be sitting under Bishop Freak Nasty, that will tell you to do whatever it takes to please one another. Well, I'm just going to leave that alone altogether. A man will be very pissed that his wife's pastor is dictating what happens in their love chambers. Trust me. That's a man who will never go to church with you. No man, especially a black one, wants his bed to be controlled by another man, whether he's a bishop, the Pope, or whoever. Now I'm not saying you cannot ask your pastor for advice, but their voice should not be the leading voice concerning your bedroom. I believe you're grown and wise enough to sit down with your companion and have a nice conversation about love making between the two of you. It's the same with your father or father figure. His voice should not be the leading voice when it comes to satisfying your companion. Some fathers can have the best intentions in all the world. Why ask one man, when you can ask the one you're sharing your life with? I'm not discouraging any woman from talking to your father, but let's get one thing clear. You didn't marry your daddy, you married 'big daddy'. Lol.

Trust me when I tell you, you'd be surprised what you can learn to love when it's with the one you love. Connecting with someone you love who is as stubborn as a mule and not open to new things can be quite challenging. I once heard a lady say that when she gets married, she'll never go down on her husband because she's not that kind of lady. I was shocked! I said to myself, you better marry a man that doesn't desire that. Some say, most men do.

I'm sure I'm not the only one that has been there before. I've tried some strange foods and went to some odd places that I myself would have never experienced, but because it was with someone I love, I was up for the challenge. That's the way it is even in lovemaking. Give the man a chance, because if you love him that much, you would at least try. Aren't they worth it?

Chapter Six

You are damaged goods from your last relationship(s) and it shows.

- *You need time to heal.*

- *Stop talking bad about your ex.*

- *Marriage is not one of your requirements.*

- *You are content being single especially after all the hell you've been through.*

To be 'damaged goods' is a very dangerous way to be. I was watching a show on TV about animals, specifically lions and such. It talked about how lions only go after wounded animals because as long as they are wounded, they are not at their full strength. When you are damaged goods, you become susceptible as prey by men because they see that. Some men look for women who they can tell are hurt and just got out of a bad relationship. And do know, he's looking for these types at the job, library, club, and church. Predators are not just beasts in the jungles of Africa and Asia, but predators are cruel men who are waiting for an opportunity to pounce on an unsuspecting suspect. You see, these type of men need these type of women to feed their insecurities and gaps in their own character. It's your credit that he wants to destroy because he has none of his own. It's your car he needs to drive because he doesn't have one. And of course, last but not least, it's your house he needs to stay at because he's homeless.

Have you ever noticed that you can buy a product from the store that has been damaged for almost half the price of the same product that is undamaged? What I'm saying is that damaged goods are never worth the full price. Some men know this, and they're not willing to put in the work that it takes to get that woman at that top shelf price. He knows deep down inside, that the average woman would not stand for his bull crap, so therefore he needs a wounded soldier. Just don't let that be you. Get healed and get whole so you can be better for yourself and those around you, especially if you have children. Can you imagine how crazy it is for a child to grow up and see his mother being treated like trailer trash by a man? To see his mother giving up everything from her body, to her hard-earned cash, can tear up the mind of an adolescent child. What message does that send to the next generation? If it's a daughter, she could grow up to accept bad behavior from a man that hardly puts anything into the relationship, but takes everything out of it. Healing is certainly of necessity and therapeutic to any woman that's been through hell. I understand now more than ever why some women walk around mad at the world, depressed, and with a bad attitude. They have been through some of the worst seasons of their lives with no end in sight. This can cause them to walk around taking it out on everybody else around them. All she needs to do is be healed. It doesn't matter how good that man looks and how much you desire that relationship if you know that you are tore-up from the inside and are damaged goods. Get healed because the relationship will go much smoother in the end.

You can want to be in a relationship so bad that you'll look past the fact that you're hurting. I've heard crazy statements such as, "A woman like me needs a man at all times." In other words, it's normal for some women to have a man no matter what. Regardless of what else is happening right or wrong in their lives, they simply believe they should have a man at all times. I heard one sister on the east side say, "Forget all that mess! Ain't nothing like a shoulder to cry on and a dick to ride on!" What in the world? Buckwild! Yes, some women are crazy and actually think like that! This is the furthest from the truth. There are times that a person should be by themselves, simply to get themselves together. You must exude maturity and understand that it's not how you are viewed in the eyes of people, but it's how you are viewed even in your own eyes.

"Girl he's not about nothing, he's not a real man, he doesn't have good credit, he's driving his mama's car, he can't even put it down in the bedroom!" These are the words of some women use when they are dogging their ex's out. All of those things may actually be true, but how does that make you look after you've been with him for the last five years? What you are really saying is you have accepted his behavior and are alright with it, especially if you were with him for a long duration of time. Please, please, please my friend, whatever you do, stop trashing your ex's name and go on and live the beautiful life that God has ahead of you. To men, when a woman keeps talking about her ex and putting him down, all she is doing is showing that new man how she's going to speak of him if their relationship doesn't work out the way she desires. All of us can point out the bad things in our last relationship, but only the mature can point out the good things in their past relationship, even though things didn't work out.

I find it quite rewarding when a woman can admit what she did wrong in the relationship and refuses to recycle that behavior. She is actually learning from her own mistakes, instead of just pointing out all the issues with the man. My kind of girl! One of the quickest ways to slow down the process of your own individual healing is to focus on the issues and the problems of your companion and never your own. When you deal with you, you get a whole lot better. Therapy at it's finest!

You'd be surprised at how many women are content with being single. These are the ones that have a man living with them and sometimes he doesn't take out the trash, doesn't clean up, he doesn't cut the grass, and they're cool with it. He has no aspiration on asking her hand in marriage. She has no problem with his lackadaisical behavior. You know why? Because he knows she's okay with being single.

Her mama, girlfriends, and everyone that truly loves her looks at her after being with the same man for years and years and asks her what's her problem is? Little do they know or realize that she's content living "common-law." And guess what friends, that's alright if that is her desire. One thing that will really clarify things, is if she told them she does not desire marriage. Of course, to others, she's bucking up against the American way because she's content with living "common-law" with her dude. But what's fair is what has been agreed on. And guess what? Sometimes you can agree without even having the discussion. It's called a nonverbal agreement. The two don't talk about it because they know what it is.

The sad thing of it is when a decade or two goes by and one dies the other is left with nothing but the bills. Nothing legally gives him or her their earthly possessions and that's when things get nasty with the opposing person's family. Though some states would say if they live a certain amount of time together that they are married and in that case, everything changes.

We should all be clear on the perspectives that are in our culture. Some women are fine being by themselves. Of course, society has its way of pushing marriage and relationships on everybody, but why do what society dictates and not what you want? What makes this thought limited, is that the majority of women appear to want to be married or in relationships, but certainly not all. There are several different reasons why some women choose to remain solo and that is their right. Some have been through so much hell with men that they just want a couple years off to get their sanity back. You'd be shocked how much a bad relationship can take out of you. It can cause you to lose faith in people, lose body weight, lose your job, and almost lose your damn mind! Some people have come into our lives, almost as if they were sent on a special assignment by the devil himself to drive us crazy! Now when I hear a woman saying, "I'm fine by myself and I'm enjoying my singlehood," I no longer do a double take when I look at her. I understand that a woman can have a list of reasons from the bottom of the floor, to the top of the ceiling. You can never judge a book by its cover. Happily single and happily divorced people are doing good all by themselves and there's nothing wrong with it.

Chapter Seven

You're full of drama and have too much attitude aka Ms. Drama & Stacy Attitude.

- *Misplaced affections*
- *Attitude determines altitude*
- *Black women and reality TV*
- *Stop telling your business on social media*

You have too much drama! A real man is a man of peace. When he gets home from a hard day's work, he doesn't want to hear you and your girlfriend on the phone trashing your bestie. Sometimes it's not even your own personal drama, but the girls that you hang around. They're always speaking down about somebody like they're all the way up. Always talking about the latest gossip. They know whose marriage is failing and whose is thriving. They know who slept with who. I mean they know everything and have mouths that are like typewriters that never stop. Trust me when I tell you, a real man is allergic to that. You will drive him away as far as the east is from the west. The Bible talks about how a man will go outside of his house and climb up on the top of his roof when it comes to dealing with a woman like that. He'd rather be in that position than sitting in the love chair in his living room or family room. Instead of watching the game, he wants to get away from a woman like that. Drama queens and motor-mouthed women are like kryptonite to Superman. Drama follows these type of women like smoke behind a city bus! You can turn away a man very quick by being a woman full of drama.

Now here's the flip side. Some women will say "Well, I'm a woman and I talk more than men. This is the way God made us." My sister, I certainly agree, but talking all the time about nothing and being full of drama, are two totally different things. We men, know that there's a time for all things. One of the greatest moments of silence to a man is when he gets in from a hard day's work and is stressed out. That's not the time to talk his head off his shoulders about nothing, especially drama and foolishness.

Misplaced affections are when an individual at times is mad over one thing, but it has nothing to do with another. For example, a man that loses his job will come back home arguing with the wife and the kids. He's taking it out on them because he lost his job. I find this quite common at times not just with women but people in general. But today, I'm talking about women. Sometimes it's because that man won't pay child support and she just gets an attitude with everybody because of what he's not doing. A woman being filled with emotions can sometimes be led by her emotions and that can be a dangerous thing.

My mom used to always tell me that a woman who can master her emotions is a powerful creature because very few can. It takes a special kind of man to be able to be with a woman whose emotions are up and down like a roller coaster at the state fair. Now I'm no fool, I know as a man women cannot contain and hold back their emotions like men. But to be able to have some sense of control is an awesome thing. Say what you want, but I don't believe a forty-year-old woman should act like an eighteen-year-old woman when she gets mad. I remember when I was a young man, I would see my mom get mad at my dad. But she was so smooth with it, that you couldn't even really tell she was mad. I guess being around her so much I had the inside track. I knew that she was mad but she didn't do anything to show it. She didn't yell, she didn't scream, she didn't tear nothing up, but deep down inside, when I looked at her, I knew something pissed her off. She just had that I don't know, I guess I call it "mad grace." A lot of older seasoned women back then had that. Probably your momma too. I would say to myself "Boy when my Dad gets back he is going to get it." Lol.

I must say this when speaking of attitudes because all of us have them, it's not just women. When something rough has happened to us, it's hard not to have an attitude. I'll never forget when I got divorced. I was one angry man. I was angry, I was bitter, I was cold. For a certain period in my life, I was hostile towards the opposite gender. My divorce had knocked me flat on my back. I was trying to hold it together like a man with gorilla glue in one hand and masking tape in the other. But it just didn't work. The rejection sent me spiraling out of control. The lawyers tore me apart and it ended up costing me $50,000 plus. I wasn't just emotionally broke, but I was financially broke too!

What a jacked up feeling that was. Talking about a mad somebody. I was on fire! Back then, if you looked at me too long I was ready to clap back. I wanted revenge on the whole female population. I know it sounds crazy, but I want to be as honest as I can. I learned way back then, that going through relationship pain can garner a long lasting bad attitude in a person if you let it. Trust me, I know how it feels when I see women go through a love TKO. One bad man that crushed your heart, slept with your sister, slapped you, gave you a venereal disease while married, not to mention tore up your credit, can crush you! Whew! That's enough to drive someone crazy and send you over the edge. I'm talking about coo-coo for cocoa puff crazy! So I understand when I see the woman in her house shoes and a gang bandana on at the grocery store with the look in her eye saying, ninjah, don't say nothing to me! I'm here for some cereal for my babies, being that their sorry daddy isn't helping, so I couldn't care less how I look! Yes, ma'am my sister! I totally understand. Just let me reach past you and get the Pop Tarts and I'll be right out of your way! Lol. Lord knows this brother understands. As a matter of fact, let me pause and take a minute to applaud women that have been through their biggest storms, toughest battles, and darkest nights, yet you smiled your way through it! You've shaken off a bad attitude you once had and are now ready for your best days, I salute you! I dare say, that in my opinion, women can go through trouble far better than us men. I mean, I've never read in the Bible that women were emotionally stronger than men. Actually, one scripture called women the weaker vessel! Yet, I've seen with my own eyes…my mother, my sisters, and even some women that I've brought problems to, recover like no other. Men would have started drinking and driving, fighting over a parking space, or blowing up on the job over the same issues women deal with. Yet, that woman cries all night long and soaks her pillow, but yet gets back up the next day to do it all over again. You, my sister, are something special! For all of those that can go through hell and still smell and look like Heaven, you are definitely next in line for a blessing!

Attitude is everything when you're going through your darkest hours. It is at that time, that one will determine their altitude. One individual said, it's not what you go through, but it's how you go through while going through. I don't know an individual alive, that when they went through something, that didn't cause a bad attitude to come upon them but there are some people are masters at this. You will never know what they are going through unless they sat you down and told you.

That attitude will creep out on social media as well. That pompous flair that says, "I am me and after all the hell I've been through, I'm going to say and do what I want." That can be very dangerous. It has done a good job at killing the image of good black women. Stroll through Facebook, Twitter, and Instagram, and you can see it clearly for yourself. The number one picture for some women is their butt! Eighty percent of their pictures are duck lips and their behind! If a man is interested in you, trust and believe he's checking out your page. If the only thing you show on your page is your backside, don't get mad if all he wants to do is smash! Some never talk about their job, their children, their family, or any other interest. Then, the first thing they say is men only want me for my body. But if that's all you are advertising, can you really get mad? Men are voyeurs and are greatly moved by what they see. Wouldn't it be better if he saw her talking about business moves or see that she's making changes toward her future? Inspiring quotes of how she rebounded from a horrid past and the joys of smiling after enduring pain! Who knows, maybe they're just showing what they think is the beautiful parts of themselves, which is their body. Maybe they think their mind, soul, and spirit is ugly, and crushed beyond measure, after all they have been through. Showing what I know will get me some attention because I don't feel that attractive anyway. The more men tell me, maybe I'll get my groove back is what some women say to themselves. You'd be surprised at what's circulating in a person's mind. Also, the need for attention is insatiable in some women.

Please stay off all social media when you are hurt, mad as hell, and frustrated. Once you say it or post something crazy, it'll make you look very dumb quoting a scripture the next day! People will know you were upset and in your feelings. Then a few days later, you have to come on and apologize and give us a retraction. Think before you press that post or send button my dear. One woman made a complete one hour video talking about all the hell that she had gone through with her baby's daddy and everything he did to her. I really felt sorry for her because she was crying, snot was coming out of her nose, and on top of all that, the woman was driving. Wow! She was getting pity from all of her friends who were saying that they were praying for her and very sorry that she had to go through what she had to go through. It was obviously a moment of weakness for her and I too felt saddened for her. I can imagine all of the vulture men that blew up her inbox and invited her out for a meal or a drink. Not one of her female friends told her to pull over and they were coming to help her.

You'd be surprised at who is attracted to your misery. They'll watch you suffer and won't lift a finger to help you. Yeah, you may get one or two offering prayer and a warm conversation, but you have to be very, very careful when you're vulnerable. You become an extremely easy target. Hundreds, if not thousands, saw you put all your business out to the public view and that's not a good thing. In my personal studies, what I enjoy the most about eagles, is that when they are in their weakest state they fly to a high, high mountain away from the public view and other birds that could catch them in their vulnerable season. They're all alone at their weakest moment. I learned a whole lot from that and I believe you should too. The light of pity is all on you at this time and if you're ever outside in the dark you will see that even night bugs are attracted to the street pole lights. I would hear old ladies sit among themselves and talk and say, "Don't let your left hand know what your right hand is doing." What that simply meant was, because you are weak, broken, hurt, and vulnerable, you don't let everybody see what you're going through. That's old school big mama talk right there.

Chapter Eight

Fine but don't have a dime

- *Don't expect him to have what you don't have.*
- *A man doesn't want a broke woman either.*
- *Finance without romance is a nuisance!*
- *You're broke with no change ($) in sight!*

Have you ever heard of the saying "romance without finance is a nuisance?" I certainly have. Women like to know that a man has his stuff together financially. My mother would tell me women are innately born like that. They like to know that a man can provide and there's nothing wrong with that. But at the same time, it can work both ways. Unfortunately, you have some women today that desire for a man to have a house, job, car, and his own business, while they themselves have none of those things. That ain't right. I know that women are more focused on a man being financially stable and nothing is wrong with that. Yet let me add to this. Why be so hard on the man to be fully established, when you yourself aren't?

Just like a woman does not want a broke man that doesn't have anything, neither do men want a broke woman that doesn't have anything. If you have none of those things, to me it would seem that you would not be so hard on the man who does not have his stuff together. If you are working a nine-to-five and make only a few bucks over minimum wage, how can you demand the man make six figures? He has to have his own house, yet you are sharing an apartment with your sister and are late on the rent every month. C'mon fam!

There's nothing more attractive to men than to see a woman who has her own. She may not be getting child support from her baby's father or help from the government, yet she grinds and makes it happen some way somehow. Now I'm not saying that she has to have all those things she wants him to have, but to see a woman grinding her way to the top, getting her degree, cleaning up up credit, shoot, that's more attractive than long hair with curls! Simply put, it would be nice to be more sensitive to a man that does not have those things, but yet he is working to get himself together. Show a little mercy if you see he's trying. Now if he's a straight-up bum and not trying to acquire anything, you should run the other way!

A man wants a wife that will be a help meet, NOT a dependent. My mom used to tell me, "The right woman will pull you all the way up. But the wrong woman will drag you all the way down!" Whew. That's what you call the raw truth. Tell me my friend, what do you think is more attractive to a man? A woman that gets her hair, nails, and eyebrows done every two weeks for $250, or a sister that has $10k in her savings account and no credit card debt? Don't take my word for it, ask a man of distinction. Hands down, it'll be a woman who is financially astute. A woman who is frivolously spending and trending on Twitter, won't catch the eye of a man who has his finances together. Brothers will take a sister with a neat ponytail than a woman with hair down to her butt trying to emulate Beyonce, but broke! Debt is killing some women that feel the need to look a part, trying to get the attention of men. You have to bring more to the table than an appetite. Men want a woman who is an asset, not a liability. Whether you choose to believe it or not, most men of astute nature will never marry a woman without first looking at her credit report. I know I won't!

One of the biggest keys about this thought is this. The woman does not have to have all of those things such as a house, car, her own business, and multiple homes around the country, but to have a woman with potential means a lot to men. In other words, she doesn't have it yet but if you look at where she's at right now, you can tell that she's working to get it together. She's in a housing program that helps her to get her own home in a few years. She's paying off old college loans and medical bills. She may be working a job which garners promotions as her skills increase or she may be in college right now working toward her first degree. All of those, are signs that she doesn't have it yet, but she's doing what it takes it to get it.

The society that we are in now, especially in the church, women expect a man to come and get her out of all of her financial woes. She's at a revival waiting for the prophet to call her out saying a millionaire is going to marry her. Really? Lol. So sad. In other words, her knight in shining armor who's coming to save her is really a brother coming to the hood to deliver her from financial woes and pay all her bills and support her without her doing anything. That is absolutely ludicrous!

How would women look at men who thought the same way? The man who's working down at a warehouse making $2 more than minimum wage, jacked up credit, no house, no car, and living with his momma, but yet in his mind he wants a woman to come and save him? That wouldn't be right and no woman I know would like that. It would show that man doesn't have initiative to do better, but simply waiting for a fool…I mean a woman, to deliver him out of his mess. My sisters, ask yourself this. Would you stay in a marriage, where your husband was ruining you continually, financially?

Running up the credit cards, not paying bills you thought were paid, sneaking new outfits into the house, finding them in the closet every weekend? Lights and cellphones being shut off, and the bank wants to foreclose? Would you, could you, stay in a relationship like that? I'm sure you wouldn't!

Men love to hear stories of a woman with potential. A woman that may have started on the bottom but she rose to the top. She had to work at Walmart during the day, but went to college at night. Yes, she has two children that her family would babysit at night to help her out. She didn't graduate in the scheduled four years, but it took her six years. Yet she graduated cum laude or shall I say oh lawdy! Lol. That's what you call a woman with great potential. Women have been doing that since the beginning of time and there are so many I see that are doing that even right now. You go girl! That's the kind of woman I'm talking about! I close this chapter with this. Gold diggers are very much still in the land, male and female. Be sure you don't end up with one, or you will be one sad individual. How can two walk together, except they agree.

Chapter Nine

You are not the marrying type.

- *Men date loose women but they'll never marry them!*
- *Whatever you do don't give it up on the first date!*
- *Girl who taught you how to do that?*

It's unfortunate that I may be forced to convince some of you of this, but let me just go ahead and say what I have to say. We know that there are all types of females, just like they are all kinds of men. There are certain women, that men talk about in the locker room at the gym. They talk about this kind of women at the pool hall. They tell the homies about all of their sexual excursions with them. That kind of woman is **ONLY** talked about in a sexual connotation. They will take this kind of woman to the movies, take her out to eat, and even out of town, but because the whole relationship is built on sex, they will never marry her. You have some women today that think their sex is so good and that's all it takes to get a husband. They act like milk and honey is flowing out of their stuff and everybody else's is dry! They will believe no different. They are absolutely wrong. They believe their sexual experience will hook a man. That is the furthest from the truth! Maybe you have, but I have never heard a man say, I'm marrying her because her stuff is so so good. I've never heard a man say I'm marrying her because sexually she takes me to the moon and back. I have never heard a man say, I'm marrying her simply because she can do that thing better than any woman I've ever been with! If he's a man of excellence, not just another freak, he will NEVER marry you because of sex that's the bomb! Let me add balance to this statement. A woman that knows how to put it down in the bedroom, will always be a plus. But it will never be the primary reason that the man goes out and puts that diamond on her left hand. Trust me sisters when I tell you this. Trust me, trust me, trust me! I, like most brothers, love me some fried chicken. But as much as I love it, I don't want to eat it every single day. What I'm saying is, no matter how good it is or how good you think it is, he will get used to it and that alone won't hold him. Genuine love has got to be there somewhere. What if you have a sickness or accident that prevents you from sexually pleasing him? What will you do then? Think about it. Life has a way of showing you what you really have when it comes to relationships. We've all seen it far too many times.

I was at the gym a long time ago, talking with some fellas

and one of them talked about a woman he really liked. The compatibility and everything was there, but there was one big problem. He had sex with her the first day he met her!! He said he could never marry her, because she probably did that with most men she met. She gave it up on the first date. The fellas tried to convince him that she might not be a loose woman, especially being that they went to a bar and had drinks, but he just couldn't shake the thought of her possibly doing that with all men. Adult beverages, I believe, have destroyed many possible relationships that could have really worked out. It causes you to be impaired and operate outside of your normal self. He couldn't move past it and that relationship ended before it could ever get started. He admitted it was partially his fault because she wanted to see a movie after dinner, but he wanted to talk and he chose the bar. Our choices can bless us or curse us.

Sex is so loose today. It seems like it's the norm when dating. It's almost expected after a date ... especially if dinner was over $75! Sex will destroy a good relationship.... especially if it's too soon. Once the female starts to think they are in a real relationship and starts acting and talking like they are a couple, he will slam on those brakes like a truck driver on the highway! In his mind, he's thinking stop tripping girl! You know you just my freak! I have a female friend that said she has never been with her dude in the daytime! Never. And they were in a relationship for a year. Now, that's a hot mess and a 'booty' relationship. No more no less!

I'll never forget years ago, I was walking through the mall with a new female friend that I was digging. We were really starting to feel one another and our compatibility was getting better and better. But the weirdest thing happened, that I had never experienced and I can't just make this up. I promise you at least five different guys spoke to her with a sinister grin! They playfully talked, and body language never lies to those of us that took the class! Don't let anybody fool you when you're in your 30s and 40s, and Lord help 50s, nobody is trying to marry the neighborhood freak! Male or female. Exclusivity will never go out of style! Just keeping it real!

Chapter Ten

He likes peanut butter and jelly!
Simply put—he's gay or bisexual!

This is a subject that many don't want to talk about because it is very taboo in the black community. Today you have black men that have deviant sexual appetites, to the point that they no longer want women, but men. Sometimes both! It's nothing old, it's nothing new, it simply is what it is. Yet when it comes to marriage, you can't act like it's not happening. Ladies don't have your eyes 'wide shut' on this subject. Don't be a fool when it comes to gay men. They will kick it with you, go to the movies with you, go out to eat with you, and at times even sleep with you. Some get down like that, but they will not marry you because they are gay. They know deep down inside that they like men, so they will not waste your time or theirs. And guess what? You should respect that. It's crazy that I even have to say this, but we are in a time and day now where you have women that are so desperate for a man that they will even take a gay man. You know I'm not lying! It seems to me that there is some type of inseparable bond that is between gay men and women…and the hair salon is the breeding ground of it. They are literally the best of friends to the end and seem to be closer friends than two women. They hang out like that old girlfriend TV show Laverne & Shirley. They go get manicures and pedicures together as well as get their hair done too. Like two peas in a pod they are inseparable. I don't know what it is but they have a strong connection. Yet a connection and a marriage are two totally different things.

When it comes to bisexual men, this is almost a complete and totally different subject. The reason why I say this is because they can hardly be detected. They are not feminine, neither do they have high squeaky voices. A lot of them look just like straight men and act just like straight men. You will have to have wisdom and street knowledge like no other. The average woman, I've been told, can't even detect a bisexual man. The only way you would know it is if he voluntarily told you. This is a dangerous game that is being played with the hearts of women, by men who have their own desires at heart. To find out that you are sleeping with a man, who sleeps with other men, is something that can make a woman have a nervous breakdown. But it is happening all the time, more than you ever know. I blog all the time on social media and I'll never forget what a disgruntled lady inboxed and told me. She said that she was mad as hell at her fiancé because he called off the wedding a week before they were to be married. I asked why in the world would he do such a thing? She said because he told her that he knew he still loved sleeping with men and thought marriage would change him. He ultimately realized it wouldn't. Wow! "I hate him!" she said. I instantly asked why would she be mad. She may hate him today, but in the years to come she would appreciate him. He could have kept his feelings to himself and walked down the aisle with her. All the while, knowing that he has a desire to sleep with men. He actually did her a favor. He could have jacked her life up beyond recognition but he saved her from a life filled with pain. You might not agree with this but I actually I applaud the brother. Why? Because he was honest. Do you know how many men lie and deceive women like this and go ahead and just get married anyway? Yet they have a cell phone filled with different brothers numbers that they will continue to sleep with. So sad on behalf of the women.

I even had a friend whom we'll call Vanessa. She was a very beautiful woman, good job, owned her home, owned a business and everything. I mean she had it all together. This kind of woman could literally get any kind of man she wanted. Yet she fell in love, or shall I say she fell in trouble with a bisexual. She really felt that this man that she was kicking it with would choose her if she kept doing all the right things. She really told me and others that her stuff (you know what I'm talking about) was so good that she can turn him away from a man. Wow! That's a challenge for you! Let me say this and I'm not trying to sound like a preacher. If God can't change him neither can you! What makes you think what's between your legs can change him? You need to really think long and hard if you have the same attitude and concept like this chick Vanessa. But that's just simply my little ole' opinion.

Let me make it clear I'm not making these statements to put any gay or bisexual man down period because I'm not their judge, jury, nor their God. That's between them and the master. I'm simply saying don't look for a man that doesn't like what you have to put a ring on your finger. It will never happen. For example, and this may be extreme, but I want to be crystal clear on a subject like this; I have been to many zoos around the country—the Bronx Zoo, the Los Angeles Zoo, even the world's famous Columbus, Ohio Zoo. Those monkeys look so cute! Some of the female monkeys even wear clothes, painted nails, and one monkey had on jewelry! Lol. But no matter how good that female monkey looks there's nothing in the world that's going to make me change my desire for a woman and lean toward that monkey. She may be smart and submissive willingly eating all the bananas and peanuts I give her at the zoo but I don't want no monkey!

Lol. And its simply because my desire is for a woman not a monkey. Just like the bisexual or gay man. His desire is for a man. Whether he's gay or a enjoys a woman every now and then, it is the raw truth whether you choose to accept it or not. He want's a man!

Chapter Eleven

He's a player! At this time of his life all he wants to do is play.

- *Stop trying to change him because he'll only change when he's ready.*
- *If you play his game be sure you know the rules.*

You guys go out to eat all the time, kick it at the movies monthly, and even have sex casually, but you'll notice he never refers to you as his woman when introducing you to his friends. Why? Because he is playing. And guess what? Nine out of ten times he has said that. If he told the woman he doesn't want to marry anyone or be no woman's boyfriend, is that a problem? The man is being totally honest. Let me take it further. What woman would want to make a man marry her when you know upfront his true intentions? Any man or woman has the right to decide if they want to marry or play. You see, play can mean different things to different people. Some want to just meet different people, go out to eat and explore their possibilities of just being friendly. Playing doesn't mean having sex with everyone you meet. Just being free is how some men want to be. Companionship is the last thing on his mind. Nothing more, nothing less. Know this if he is living the lifestyle of a player, getting intimate with him can cause some serious issues. You can find yourself on the sidelines having so called booty remorse! I think you know what that means. It's one thing to buy something in the store and you get home and change your mind about it. You are having what is called buyers remorse. You have the product intact and your receipt so you can take it back. But once you give up your body, there is no getting that back. Booty remorse is nothing to play with because you only have one body.

Herein lies the problem. Some women think that when she meets this player he's going to see how awesome a woman she is and they're going to be in a relationship. She says to herself, "I'm not worrying about all those other women he's seeing because once he get's with me it's just a matter of time!" No, my dear, with the player it doesn't work like. If he has told you and continues to tell you that he want's to be single, believe him! Do know this above all. Him meeting you and dating you does not make you the awesome woman that you are! You have to know that at all times because if you don't you will think there's an inadequacy in you when it's not. I can't tell you how many female friends I know struggle intensely in this area. Because the player doesn't choose you,

you think something's wrong. Absolutely nothing is wrong. Actually, everything is going right. He's only doing what he told you. I dare say if you find yourself falling in love or getting in too deep and he keeps pulling out his player's card in conversation, you might have to take a step back. You have to guard your heart at all times and sometimes even from yourself. King Solomon said in the book of Proverbs "Guard your heart above all else, for it determines the course of your life." Notice it is nobody else's job to guard your heart and make sure you don't get caught up in something. If you my sister can master this you will become a bad somebody! Women that don't guard their hearts usually become that player's stalker. He doesn't understand why she scratched up the side of his car with a screwdriver. He is shocked that she's in his bushes by the garage when he went to take out the trash! He doesn't know why in the world she's calling up the other women he's dated and sabotaging his name. He's told her dozens of times, but not realizing it's going in her left ear and coming out of her right ear. In her mind, he belongs to her, which is the furthest from the truth. She should have guarded her heart because it's her job, not his. Remember he thinks she's cool with his life choices, and if not, the average woman would have been spoken her mind. When she saw herself falling deeper and deeper in love with him, to the point she doesn't think she can live without him, it's time to abort that situation. If you find yourself fantasizing about him all day to the point you can't focus on your own affairs, get up out of that. When things don't end the way you want, you can find yourself on the edge of a nervous breakdown for real. It has happened and will continue to happen to so many women who lost control of their heart. Just be sure it doesn't happen to you.

There will always be that one woman that is set out on changing him. And guess what, it happens more not often. Women love projects and they love to influence a situation and that's okay. Yet it can be extremely stressful trying to change a man into marrying her when he's a player. She'll find herself getting mad when he talks with or goes out with other women. She'll follow him on social media and observe his interactions with other females trying to detect if he's in a relationship with them. She begins to slowly turn into a security dog, protecting what she thinks is her property. In her mind, he's her property because she's assigned to change his mind. At least that's what she's convinced herself! That man will change only when he's ready. The woman that keeps trying to change him will eventually turn him off. If he's a sensible man he doesn't want to hurt her. You have to understand if he told her numerous times that he doesn't want to be in a relationship, he is not leading her on. I can hear some of you now saying, "Oh yes he is!" Players are going to play, that's what they do and the sooner you understand that, the better you will know how to deal with him...if at all.

If you know he's a player and decide to play, be sure you know the rules. Let's get this on quick. What are the rule you ask? There are none!! The player is going to do whatever he want's and with whomever he wants. This is a crazy game. He'll go to the movies, out to eat, even out of town with whomever he wants. And check this out...as long as he's being upfront and direct with the women he deals with, they don't have a problem with it. Some of them that is. Don't you realize how many women are doing the same thing? I digress. In our culture, so many women are open to sharing a man! Yep I said it. He belongs to none but is friends with them all. What is challenging about this game is that some men can date different women for years never desiring to marry any of them. This has to be understood by women who are going to play this game with him because not every woman can do this. Some women can't hang around a man for years without a future together in site. Now notice I said some not all. There are some women that can do the exact same thing with no problem. Believe me when I tell you that. We are in a totally different culture than just ten years ago. A player usually will keep playing until he meets the right woman.

Chapter Twelve

He's already married!

- *The kind of woman that wants what she's not supposed to have.*
- *The thirst is real.*

- *Leave that married man alone.*

Now, I know I'm already going to get in trouble for this but it's the truth. Never in all my years have I seen so many women that literally target married men. I mean, it is literally like a turn on for these type of women to go after a man that is already taken. Now it appears that that wedding ring has now become a magnet when it should have been a stay away signal. You have women that would stoop so low to where they don't mind sharing a man. They defiantly say that sharing a man is better than having no man at all. My goodness. These kind of women who have this type of mentality, really just want a man that's already taken so she doesn't have to have that much responsibility with him. Have you noticed the chick on the side usually doesn't have to cook his food and wash his clothes but mainly she's just there for companionship and sex. The fact of the matter is, she really never will know him like his wife knows him because the wife sees all sides of him. The side chick is his relaxation and relief piece, at her place, especially when he gets into arguments with his wife. She's his getaway. A place where he can show his good side and never have to reveal his bad characteristics. But the trap door to a situation like this never ends in happiness. Feelings get stronger and stronger and now what was fun on the weekends and late at night, the side chick wants that all the time. But nothing can happen. Why? Because he's already married. It's a dangerous thing to go after what already belongs to another because at the end of the day you always lose.

I would be dead wrong if I didn't mention this aspect of married men and single women. There are so many single women that get a bad rap because they were involved with a married man. But no one asks the question did they know he was married in the first place? There are some women who once they find out he is married, they will leave him alone. For others it's much much harder because their emotions, feelings and heart is involved, as well as a plethora of other things that are not easily seen. I'd be lying if I didn't confess that I almost got caught up with a married woman. She painted her husband so bad like he was Satan's nephew. She told me he beat her, cheated on her, and took her paychecks when she got paid. I felt the black superman rising up in me like it was my job to rescue her. But there was this thing I couldn't overlook. My mother always told me there are two sides to every story. I told her I wanted to speak to him but she kept dodging it like a bullet. That sent alarm bells off in my head and put me on high alert. I happened to bump into him at a gas station months later and what he told me flipped my wig. He said he had proof that she was sexually involved with two guys and that she knew that a divorce would give her half of his estate. He mentioned his prenuptial agreement was only for ten years then after that it would be null and void. That next month would be the ten year mark. A hot mess, I know. Boy she almost had me. She talked about him to me with real tears and snot. What an actress and what a fool I would have been trying to rescue her. Don't ever forget those two sides no matter what.

Many women have been swept off their feet by a man they had no clue he was married. He never wore a wedding ring and they literally can call or text him any hours of the day. Not to mention most cheating married men will have two cell phones! This is what you call a top-notch classic married player. They are the best in the game and you'll never catch them without the right answer or without a golden excuse. He will give you every reason in the book why he can't divorce his wife. His reasonings are like that of a college professor.

He has the best of excuses. He'll say, "I can't leave now my child is about to graduate. I can't divorce right now she's sick or pregnant. Hang in there with me a little while longer baby I just have some business transactions that I don't want her name on." He'll be so convincing as he looks you directly in your face telling a bold face lie that there's no way in the world you won't believe him. Just when he knows his grip is loosening, he'll bring you chocolate, and candy or a promising three-day trip. That's one smooth operator. Deception at its finest!

Because of this, many women have fell victim to married men, because he was so so good at his game. I honestly feel sorry for these kind of women and I have met so many of them in my travels. They are now on the sidelines sometimes having to watch him and his wife and kids go on living happily ever after. And the hard part is her inwardly saying, "I wish that was me!" But because of his deception, it's not her. You can say what you want, feelings don't turn on and off like a water faucet. Sometimes you can really be in love with a person and even if they've done something evil to you you still love them. There's really no antidote and no major precaution to give women when it comes to this because some married men are really, really that good. And hey while we're here some women or should I say some wives are that good too! The only thing that can happen in a scenario like this is when the truth is revealed to you, do the right thing. The right thing is leaving them the hell alone! No ifs, ands, or buts about it. Leave them alone! To think that they deceived you like that what else do you think they could possibly be hiding? Many women couldn't trust a person like that no further than they can throw him. That is deception on the highest level. An individual that can suck you into their world, get you hooked, looking you in the face for months, even years and be married but never tell you is wicked!

Some would say there are exceptions to the rules because there are some married people that have been separated for years, even living in different states. The only reason why they are not divorced is because they are both stubborn as Mississippi mules. Many have said that they have found no reason to divorce because they never got into a serious relationship, so why bother? Interesting. With others, they say they got involved with a married man because he is actually going through a divorce and have shown them the paperwork from his lawyer. In this day of high-tech deception, one still would be very cautious with anyone that is still legally married. Once they're fully divorced it's open season.

Believe me when I tell you this, there's nothing like planting bad seeds of disruption in someone else's marriage. You and I already know the word that says, "Whatever a man sows that he shall also reap." You can't plant apples and expect for oranges to come up at harvest time. There are so many women that would think that they are Wonder Woman with a cape and they are rescuing that man from a bad wife. But have you ever considered that he could simply be lying to you about his wife? Have you ever sat down at Starbucks and had a conversation with that wife? I'm sure it will blow your natural-born mind, hearing her version. I'm a man and I'll be the first to admit, we will say whatever we need to say to get what we want. That husband will tell you she's not feeding him, she's not washing his clothes and most of all she's not to give him no sex. But the fact of the matter is, she could be separating his whites and his dark clothes, scrubbing the skid marks out of his stank underwear by hand, loving him down to the boogie down, and cooking that man three square meals a day! You don't live in that household, so you just don't know, so never assume. I'll never forget my dad told a story one day about a married couple that were members of his church. One Sunday morning a beautiful lady came into the church. He said she was built like a brick house. After just two weeks, she began to have an affair with a woman's husband. She mesmerized this man to the point that he left his wife and family to be with her. They moved down south somewhere and sort of lived happily ever after. They even had a few children. But some twenty years later the exact same scenario happened to her. A younger more beautiful woman stole that same husband from her. That wife began to think back and wonder what went wrong in the marriage. Then it came to her what she did to that lady twenty years ago. The same thing happened to her. Don't let anybody fool you, the pendulum swings both ways and when it comes back it hit's harder and deeper.

I don't care how many dreams you had, how many visions you've seen, or even the fake prophecy from that magician… oops I mean that prophet you received, God is not the author of confusion. He will never send you somebody else's husband. Whether his wife is taking care of him or not. Remember it is never your job to get that marriage back in order. You are trespassing on dangerous ground. What goes around comes around.

Chapter Thirteen

He didn't marry you in the time you've given him.

- *Whose time table are you going by? Yours only? Why not his too?*
- *If he's still with you there is hope.*

This is the last one, but certainly far from the least. He didn't choose you to marry because he didn't marry you in the time you gave him. Now when you look at the time, who is it that dictates whether it should it be two years, three years, or five years we have to be engaged before we marry is the question? If you are driven by a time clock of your age ladies, is that really fair to the man? You may have crows feet on the sides of your eyes, graying hair, and in the chest area London Bridge is falling down! Smile. Yet, because those situations exist, does that qualify one to be married? Based on just that? What that would simply mean is if you're 40 years old, you may only want to date for two years before you married. But if you're 29, you and him can take your time. One of the things I found out that's very wrong with this type of setup, is the fact that every couple should have their own time. Sometimes the both of you can be together for a while, yet accomplishing goals. For example, you may be trying to get a four-year degree before you get married. He may still be in the military and wants to marry when he gets out. You're trying to launch your own business or get some heavy debt off your credit. The both of you should sit down and talk early in the relationship when you find out you want to be together for life, instead of what that timetable should be. That cannot be dictated by big mama, friends, or any family, for that matter. Back in grand mama's day, they would date for two or three months and then get married. You absolutely positively cannot do that in a time like today. Why you ask? Because people married today for all the wrong reasons. You have people that want to rush and get married because they need help to pay their bills. You have others that are getting married real quick because they want to become a citizen of this country. And then you also have some that want to get married simply because they want to have sex. It is absolutely crazy to marry for any of those reasons. Can you imagine dating a foreigner from a different country and they are pushing the marriage real quick because they're trying to get a green card and become a citizen? Can you imagine somebody wanting to marry you quickly because they bought a house they couldn't afford and need your financial support? Then are you really a spouse or a bill paying companion?

What about marrying somebody simply because the sex is good? That would be asinine because no matter how much you like fried chicken after awhile it gets old. What are you going to do when the both of you no longer have that high sex drive like you did when you were younger and first met? Then you have those women who have daily conversations about marriage with their girlfriends at the gym or the salon. Some, certainly not all, would say, "I'm not going to sit around and let no man waste my time. If you don't put a ring on it in two years, I'm out!" Come on girl, you know that ain't right! Don't you know that it takes different people, different times to become adjusted and compatible with each other? Are you saying, just because you've been together for two years you should marry? Imagine if that two years was filled with fighting, cussing, and not getting along? Would you still want to marry that person simply because 24 months have expired? Of course not! It's not the time together that matters, but the quality time you've had and knowing you two have been getting along. I have known couples who have been together for five years. In the five years that they've been together, they've been catching each other cheating, fighting like cats and dogs, tearing up the furniture in the house, and the list goes on. Who in their right mind would want to marry somebody after living in chaos for years? I must repeat it. It's about the quality time you've had together, not simply the length of time. You mean to tell me just because you have been with a man for three years, you want to marry him because the girls at the salon said so? You should go back and ask those same girls would they do the same thing they're telling you to do? It's very easy to tell somebody what they should do when it's not you. People have a way of putting you in a hot boiling pan, while they stand on the sidelines and watch you burn like bacon to a crisp. That ain't right! Most sensible couples will want to be sure that they are compatible with this person for a long length of time to avoid misery in the years to come. This is something that wise women won't do, unlike women who simply hear a clock ticking in their head. You see, what is actually happening here is they are being pressured from the outside-in and not from the inside out. Just like women say, that they don't want a man to waste their time, don't you think the man feels the same way too? Or is it simply your opinion that matters here and not his? Why does it simply have to be the time you set? I've known women to not even tell the man how much time they are giving him and when that time is up if they don't have that diamond on that left wedding finger, they are out like house lights that haven't been paid. I had one friend that was dating a young lady and they had their valleys and their mountain moments. Little did he know that according to her, after two years and no ring the relationship would be over. He said that she didn't even tell him that in the 24 months if he had not proposed the relationship was over. He had to come back to an apartment that was halfway cleaned out before he realized what had happened. Now that's what you call cold blooded. Once he called her, she told him she moved in with her girlfriend. He said to her, "I wish I would have had at least known that the clock was ticking like an atomic bomb." The sensible thing to do was to at least tell him how much time you are looking forward to being in a relationship before you get married.

Is it even fair for the woman to control the timetable? Doesn't that seem kind of selfish? I know many of you would say that men take much longer than women and you are right. But it should never be set by simply the woman's time and never not his as well. What if a man is dating a type of woman that he himself has a timetable too? Imagine during that time, that he's trying to decide if this is the woman to marry and he's seeing all the wrong signs? What if during the two or three years he have set he sees a woman that can't keep a house clean? Dishes piled up in the sink for weeks, trash all on the floor and the garbage can is flowing over in the kitchen and bathrooms like the Niagara Falls? What if all he sees is her feminine products laying all over the place, hair all in the sink like a Chia pet just got a haircut, and makeup smeared on the vanity mirror in the bathroom? Don't you think he too will be apprehensive about marrying a woman like that? Especially if he grew up in a home where his mother kept the house immaculate. You mean to tell me, that because years have gone by and he had to live in this, he should still just go ahead and marry this woman? Absolutely not! That may be a sign to that man that this is not the woman that I want to spend the rest of my life with. I truly believe especially after talking to a lot of my male friends that even men too have a timetable that they like to be married. They need time to see if this is the queen of my dreams or a witch riding on a broom that I need to run from. Are you still with me? Okay stay right there. Imagine if he's used to a woman that cooks dinner sometimes. Notice I said sometimes. Because I know that the demands of today's culture and society can leave her to the point that she can't cook for him every night. What if she can't cook at all? What if he's used to home cooked meals and doesn't want to order Pizza Hut, KFC or Chinese food every night? He's looking at his time slip through his fingers like sand through the hourglass. In his mind he just might be saying after all the complaining I've done and all the fussing we've had over these simple issues I thought she would have changed by now? You cannot possibly think that he should still go ahead and marry her if this is the type of environment he has to live in. I know that this scripture is not in the Bible, but Lord knows it should be. Cleanliness is definitely next to godliness! I can't speak for all men, but certainly clean men and there's no way that they can live in a unkept house by a woman that refuses to cook or clean. I hear you loud and clear saying it is certainly not just her job to keep the house clean. You are so right. Most couples that live together, expect each person to do their part. Just like he doesn't expect you to cut the grass, trim it, and sweep the sidewalk you shouldn't expect him to cook every meal and keep the inside of the house clean. Cohabiting can be a wonderful thing when you are trying to make things work out for the best. Yes, I'm glad you asked. What if the two of you live in separate households? That is even better and what some would say the right way. You get a chance to see how they live especially without you being in the house demanding certain chores to be done. If both of you live separate from each other, this is much much easier to depict. If you go over to the house and it always looks like a war zone, you are in big trouble, unless you are slob yourself. Can you imagine going over to that woman's house and everytime you go there the toilet is filled with urine? Can you imagine going over to that man's house and there are brown bombs floating around in the toilet from two days ago? Yuck, I'm out I don't know about you! Let me also add this. Don't think you are going to change a person's living habits overnight. They can be used to living like that all the time. If that person is 25 or 35 years old, remember that's how they've been living for years and your loud mouth and complaining won't change it. Trust me. We are all creatures of habit, whether they be good or bad. A person will usually do, what they have been doing. Don't forget I said that. I'll never forget, as a young man my dad used to tell the story of how one lady's husband approached him. My dad was the pastor of a small church in Harlem, NY. After service one day, he and the church bus driver, along with other members went to drop this one lady home. When they got there, her husband stormed out of the house. He immediately came to the passenger door where my father was sitting. My dad said he had a very mean look on his face. When he came over to his window the man knocked on the window very hard! My dad said, "Lord I hope I don't have to fight tonight because I'm trying to be saved especially with my members looking at me!" Lol. He reluctantly rolled down the window and said, "Can I help you sir?" The man replied, "I don't have a problem with my wife going to church, but I need you to come in and take a look at something." The wife immediately shouted, "Pastor don't pay him no mind, please just leave." Dad thought to himself? Why does this woman not want me to see what her husband wants to show me? He said something got out to see what her husband was talking about. The husband said, "I don't mind my wife supporting and going to your church sir, but you have to see how she lives in this house with me and the kids!" My dad said when he stepped in the house, he could not believe his eyes. Clothes and trash were all over the place. It looked like a bomb had exploded in every room! Dishes were flowing all out of the sink. He said it smelled like five dogs had died in there and two skunks were still on the loose! He looked at that church lady in disbelief. The next day he ordered five sisters from the church to go over there and help her clean up. They had to literally rent a dumpster for her to clean out all of the trash that was still piled up in the house. Unfortunately, that same behavior continued for months. That man eventually divorced her and moved on with his life. I'm trying to tell you, the time together doesn't matter, but the unity, harmony, and compatibility while together mean everything.

If he's still with you, there is hope for that relationship. I know many of you will absolutely positively not agree with me but trust me, men don't hang around for nothing. At least not all men. Of course, you will have those that are scared to jump the broom and will use any and every reason not to marry. Yet, there are still some men that hang around because they believe and hope that things will get better. He could have easily left a relationship and moved on with somebody else, but perhaps he's hanging around and hopes the things will change with you and him. I'm sure that this is something that you women do not want to hear, but Lord knows it's the truth. Don't take my word for it, try asking him. I myself can attest to have been in many relationships and things were going crazy, but yet my love for the woman made me hold out a little while longer. A true man will never invest his quality time and years into a woman that he has no desire to hopefully be with, in the future. One of the worst things I've seen couples do is marry the right person but at the wrong time. Remember, it may not always be that the woman is the problem, it could also be the man that's jacked. At that time in his life he's between jobs, he's broke, or he's simply trying to better himself in life. Who would voluntarily want to eat an unbaked cake that should have been in the oven just ten minutes longer? Who would willingly sink their teeth into meat that is undercooked and has blood still running out of it? Only a fool. Just like half cooked food has the potential of killing you, so will half-baked people. Don't wait all your life for a half-cooked person, but wait until they are completely done.

Conclusion

If you are already blessed with a man in your life, thank God for him and treat him like you would want him to treat you. At the same time, ask God, is this the one for you, while you yourself are checking for signs. One of the worst things I see happening today is a person wasting their time with someone that they don't see in their future. Closing doors sometimes is the only thing that opens doors. If you are a good woman, you deserve a good man. Believe that for yourself, without anyone else having to tell you. It seems to me at times, the wrong women have the husbands, and the right women are single. That's my personal observation.

It was said, that there was a huge women's conference being held on the East Coast. Hundreds, even up to the thousands of women had converged on this conference center to learn about men for the next three days. There were doctors, psychiatrists, women that had been married for 40 and 50 years, and marriage counselors. They were all giving their professional opinions on men and how women can better themselves and get along well with them. After all of these professionals gave their opinions, stories, and truths they picked up along the way, and their professional journeys, there was one last speaker. It was an old lady that had been married for sixty plus years. This old lady was known all around the world on teaching women how to treat their husbands and how to become a suitable mate for marriage. She walked up to the stage small, skinny, and frail. They adjusted the microphone stand low enough to her mouth. Mother's voice was not that loud, but oh did she have a wealth of knowledge to give. I can't tell all I heard but I'll leave you with some of the main points of this woman's speech.

Mother's 3 F's.

1. Feed him - As his wife, it is your job to feed him whenever he is hungry. He should never have to go back to his mama's house, his sister's house, or the restaurant, simply to have a good meal. Feed him at home, so he don't have to roam! Don't make him the type of husband that has to be fed by Popeye's Chicken, Wendy's, or run to the border at Taco Bell. It is your job to always feed him.

2. Don't fight him - We are in a time and day where women will fight a man and it doesn't mean anything to them. Sometimes the man is not even fighting back, but she's punching, kicking, scratching, slapping him…anything to make him fight back. But whatever you do, don't fight him. He doesn't need a fighter, but rather a lover.

3. F him! *(Use your imagination on this last one)* - Love his brains out! Simply put, if his manhood goes up, it is your job to make it go back down! Love the hell out of your man. He should never have to leave the house frustrated or mad because he did not get his sexual needs met. No matter what your job is outside of the home, remember your first job should be to him and being sure that you love and satisfy him. Sometimes you'll need to put your emotions to the side, which is very challenging for some women but you can do it. When a man is getting sexually fed at home he doesn't have to roam. Momma walked off the stage to a loud standing ovation!

There are literally so many different reasons that women think men won't get married. Yet let me flip it before I close it. Have you ever thought about the men that were turned down by women and said to themselves, "What's wrong with me? Why did she reject my engagement ring? Do I not make enough money? Why isn't my job good enough?" He's hurt too, especially if rejected publicly in front of family and friends at a surprise engagement party. Every woman that has been proposed to didn't say yes! No, I wouldn't say that we experience the same kind of pain, but rejection with men is a beast! Trust me. It even happened to me many years ago.

I thought I'd met the perfect woman. She told me we get along well and are very compatible and loved how I looked and cooked! But the occupation I have she could never conform to. Bam it was over just like that. You may call it simple or ridiculous but everybody has different ideas about what they want out of life. They're entitled to that. This is life and things will always happen to us, but things will also happen for us. I am a firm believer that whatever is destined to happen, it will happen in its own time. My desire for you today, my queens, is that you do what you feel is best to prepare yourself to become that wife. Once you've done your part, that's when things will come together. Try to never be the kind of woman that thinks she's not married because there's something wrong with men, or shall I say the men she's dated. Perhaps there could be some flaws that you have, that you don't see, and perhaps it's simply just not your time yet. We all have character flaws, some are just worse than others.

I truly believe that the knowledge, experiences, and stories I've shared with you have given you great insight on the topic, "Why he won't marry you." A guide to understanding men. What the right man well tell you and what the wrong man don't want you to find out."w

OTHER BOOKS BY JONATHAN K. SANDERS

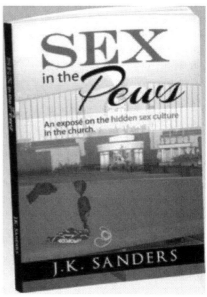

Available online @ Amazon, Barnes & Boble and
www.jksandersministries.org

Made in the USA
Lexington, KY
26 September 2017